D1195109

J
978.3
KOPP
6/14   18.30

SOUTH DAKOTA

Megan Kopp

www.av2books.com

LET'S READ

AV2
BY WEIGL™

ADDED VALUE • AUDIO VISUAL

Go to **www.av2books.com**, and enter this book's unique code.

BOOK CODE

R 6 4 0 0 0 0

AV² by Weigl brings you media enhanced books that support active learning.

AV² provides enriched content that supplements and complements this book. Weigl's AV² books strive to create inspired learning and engage young minds in a total learning experience.

Your AV² Media Enhanced books come alive with...

Audio
Listen to sections of the book read aloud.

Video
Watch informative video clips.

Embedded Weblinks
Gain additional information for research.

Try This!
Complete activities and hands-on experiments.

Key Words
Study vocabulary, and complete a matching word activity.

Quizzes
Test your knowledge.

Slide Show
View images and captions, and prepare a presentation.

... and much, much more!

Published by AV² by Weigl
350 5th Avenue, 59th Floor
New York, NY 10118
Website: www.av2books.com   www.weigl.com

Copyright ©2013 AV² by Weigl
All rights reserved. No part of this publication may be reproduced, stored in a retrieval system, or transmitted in any form
or by any means, electronic, mechanical, photocopying, recording, or otherwise, without the prior written permission of the publisher.

Library of Congress Cataloging-in-Publication Data

Kopp, Megan.
 South Dakota / Megan Kopp.
   p. cm. -- (Explore the U.S.A.)
 Includes bibliographical references and index.
 ISBN 978-1-61913-403-4 (hard cover : alk. paper)
 1. South Dakota--Juvenile literature. I. Title.
 F651.3.K66 2013
 978.3--dc23
                            2012016262
Printed in the United States of America in North Mankato, Minnesota
1 2 3 4 5 6 7 8 9 0 16 15 14 13 12

052012
WEP040512

Project Coordinator: Karen Durrie
Art Director: Terry Paulhus

Weigl acknowledges Getty Images as the primary
image supplier for this title.

SOUTH DAKOTA

Contents

3

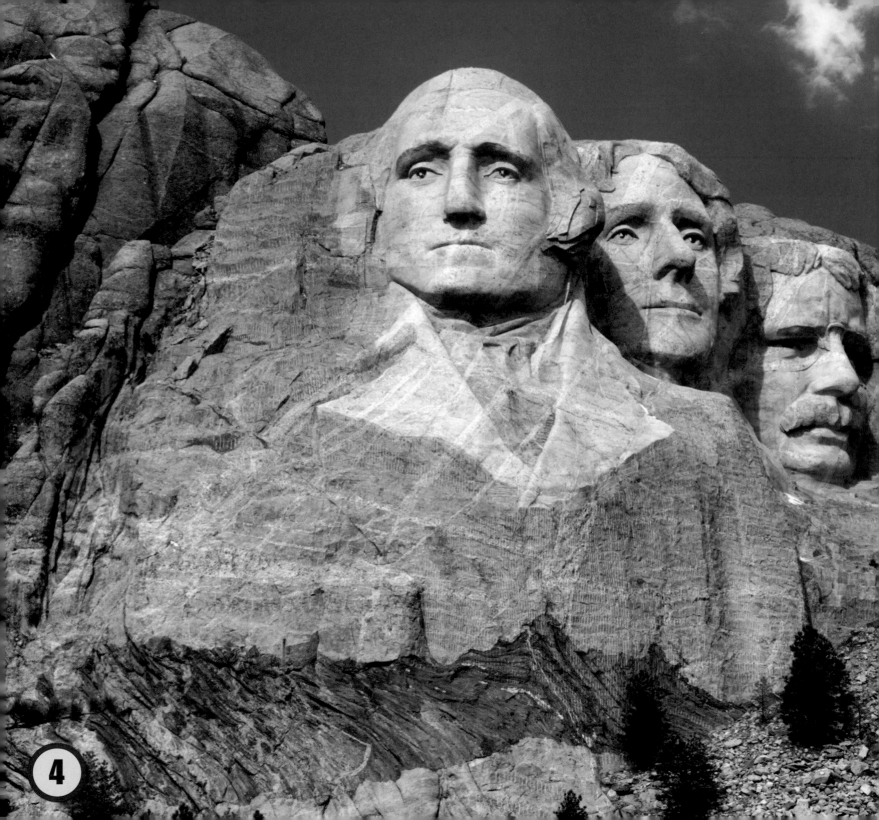

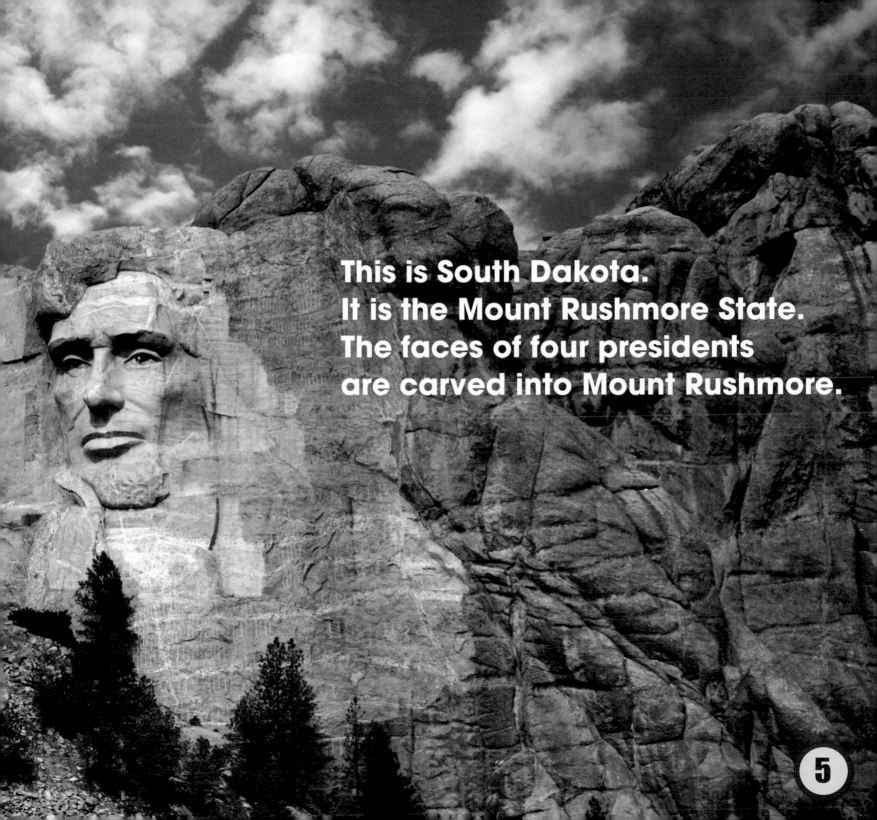

This is South Dakota.
It is the Mount Rushmore State.
The faces of four presidents
are carved into Mount Rushmore.

This is the shape of South Dakota. It is found in the north part of the United States. South Dakota is part of the Great Plains.

Where is South Dakota?

N

W   E

S

Canada

United States

Pacific Ocean

Atlantic Ocean

Mexico

Six states border South Dakota.

American Indians have lived in South Dakota for thousands of years. Settlers came to farm the land about 150 years ago.

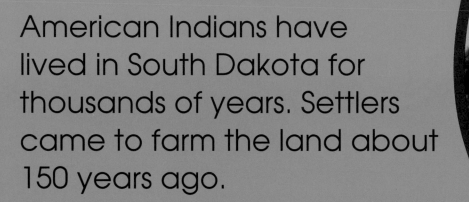

Gold was found in the town of Deadwood in 1875.

9

The purple pasque is the South Dakota state flower. It is part of the buttercup family.

The South Dakota state seal has a farmer, a boat, and cows.

STATE OF SOUTH DAKOTA
UNDER GOD THE PEOPLE RULE
GREAT SEAL
1889

The state seal also shows a mine.

This is the state flag of South Dakota. It shows the state seal and a blue sky.

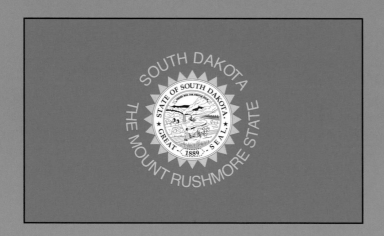

The state nickname is written around the seal.

The state animal of South Dakota is the coyote. This animal sleeps during the day and hunts at night.

Coyotes can run up to 40 miles an hour.

Pierre is the capital of South Dakota. This city is in the middle of the state.

Pierre was built near the Missouri River.

Most of the land in South Dakota is used for farms. Corn is the top crop grown by farmers.

South Dakota has more than five million acres of corn crops.

19

People come from far away to see Mount Rushmore. Some go hiking in the Black Hills.

Other people visit South Dakota to fish in its many lakes and streams.

21

SOUTH DAKOTA FACTS

These pages provide detailed information that expands on the interesting facts found in the book. These pages are intended to be used by adults as a learning support to help young readers round out their knowledge of each state in the *Explore the U.S.A.* series.

Pages 4–5

South Dakota is home to the famous Mount Rushmore National Memorial. This granite sculpture commemorates four U.S. presidents. These presidents are George Washington, Thomas Jefferson, Theodore Roosevelt, and Abraham Lincoln. The faces on Mount Rushmore stand about 60 feet (18 meters) high from forehead to chin.

Pages 6–7

On November 2, 1889, South Dakota joined the United States as the 40th state. South Dakota is part of the Great Plains region of the United States. Minnesota and Iowa are across the border to the east. North Dakota is to the north, Nebraska to the south, and Wyoming and Montana to the west. The geographic center of the United States, including Alaska and Hawai'i, is in South Dakota.

Pages 8–9

Prehistoric humans lived in the South Dakota area as far back as 10,000 years ago. European explorers arrived in the area in the 1700s. The Sioux American Indians followed bison herds into the region at about the same time. In 1817, European settlers built a settlement at the site of present-day Fort Pierre.

Pages 10–11

The pasque is related to the buttercup. The pasque is also known as the May Day Flower because its blossom is one of the first signs of spring in South Dakota. The state seal includes symbols of some of the state's natural resources. The seal features a farmer plowing his fields, a steamboat chugging down a river, and grazing cattle.

Pages 12–13

The South Dakota flag features the state seal surrounded by a golden blazing sun in a field of sky blue. South Dakota is sometimes called the Sunshine State for its big sky and sunny days. The words "South Dakota, The Mount Rushmore State" are arranged in a circle around the Sun.

Pages 14–15

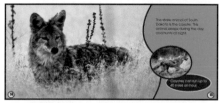

The coyote lives throughout South Dakota, though its numbers are decreasing. It is mostly nocturnal and hunts alone or in packs. Coyotes are most numerous along the Missouri River and in the Black Hills, but they also make their homes on the prairies. South Dakota is also nicknamed the Coyote State.

Pages 16–17

Pierre was first selected as a temporary capital because it is in the center of the state. Huron and Mitchell were among the towns that competed with Pierre to become the state capital. In 1904, the state legislature voted in favor of Pierre and began work on a capitol building. The building was finished in 1910.

Pages 18–19

South Dakota's farmland is one of its most important natural resources. Ninety percent of South Dakota's land is devoted to farming and ranching. Crops include corn, soybeans, wheat, and sunflowers. About 75 percent of the corn grown in the state is used for food. The rest is used to make a fuel called ethanol.

Pages 20–21

South Dakota's state slogan is "Great Faces, Great Places." About two million people visit Mount Rushmore each year. They also spend time in the Black Hills, which get their name from their dark wooded slopes. South Dakota has so many streams and lakes that it has more shoreline than the state of Florida.

KEY WORDS

Research has shown that as much as 63 percent of all written material published in English is made up of 300 words. These 300 words cannot be taught using pictures or learned by sounding them out. They must be recognized by sight. This book contains 60 common sight words to help young readers improve their reading fluency and comprehension. This book also teaches young readers several important content words, such as proper nouns. These words are paired with pictures to aid in learning and improve understanding.

Page	Sight Words First Appearance
5	are, faces, four, into, is, it, of, state, the, this
7	found, in, part, where
8	about, American, came, farm, for, have, Indians, land, lived, to, was, years
11	a, also, and, family, has, shows
12	around
15	an, animal, at, can, day, miles, night, run, up
16	city, near
19	by, more, most, than, used
21	away, come, far, from, go, its, many, other, people, see, some

Page	Content Words First Appearance
5	Mount Rushmore, presidents, South Dakota
7	Great Plains, shape, United States
8	Deadwood, gold, settlers, thousands, town
11	boat, cows, flower, mine, pasque, seal
12	flag, nickname, sky
15	coyote, hour
16	capital, middle, Missouri River, Pierre
19	acres, corn, crop
21	Black Hills, lakes, streams

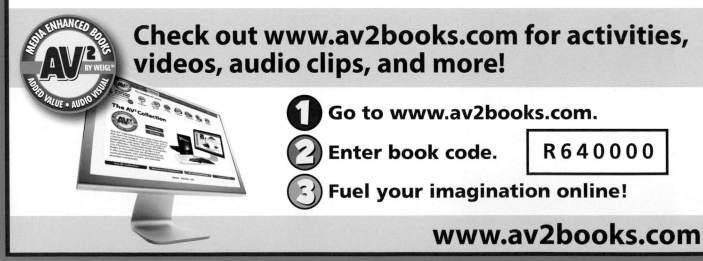

MEDIA ENHANCED BOOKS
AV² BY WEIGL™
ADDED VALUE • AUDIO VISUAL

Check out www.av2books.com for activities, videos, audio clips, and more!

1 Go to www.av2books.com.

2 Enter book code. R 6 4 0 0 0 0

3 Fuel your imagination online!

www.av2books.com

GEORGE H. & ELLA M.
RODGERS MEMORIAL LIBRARY
194 DERRY ROAD
HUDSON, NH 03051